THE STEADFAST TIN SOLDIER

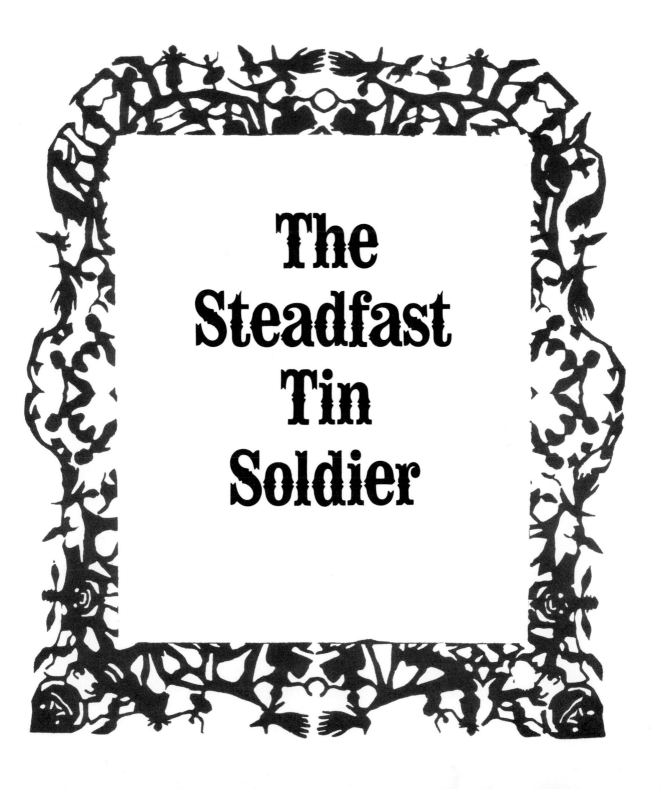

The
Steadfast
Tin
Soldier

ISBN 0-87127-125-7

Library of Congress Catalog Card Number 81-67059
Printed in the United States of America

Dance Horizons, 1801 East 26th Street, Brooklyn, N.Y. 11229

Original story of "The Steadfast Tin Soldier" reprinted
from *Hans Andersen's Stories,* newly translated;
Riverside Literature Series No. 49, Feb. 1891.
Boston; Houghton, Mifflin and Company.

On the jacket:
Judith Fugate and Mikhail Baryshnikov

The papercut borders used on jacket and
text pages are by Hans Christian Andersen.

The story of George Balanchine's
New York City Ballet production

Told in photographs by
Steven Caras

With text by
Andrew Mark Wentink

Including the Original Story by
Hans Christian Andersen

Choreography by
George Balanchine

Music by Georges Bizet

Scenery and Costumes by
David Mitchell

CONTENTS

PART I

The Story

THERE were once five-and-twenty tin soldiers; they were all brothers, for they had all been born of one old tin spoon. They held guns, and looked straight before them; their uniform was red and blue, and very fine. The first thing they had heard in the world, when the lid was taken off the box, in which they lay, had been the words "Tin soldiers!" a little boy spoke up and clapped his hands. The soldiers had been given to him, for it was his birthday; and now he put them on the table. Each soldier was exactly like the rest; but one of them was a little different; he had one leg because he had been cast last of all, and there had not been enough tin to finish him; but he stood as firmly upon his one leg as the others on their two; and it was just this soldier who became worth talking about.

On the table on which they had been placed stood many other playthings, but the toy that most took the eye was a neat castle of cardboard. Through the little windows one could see straight into the hall. Outside stood some small trees and a little looking-glass, which was made to look like a clear lake. Swans of wax swam on this lake, and looked at themselves in it. This was all very pretty; but the prettiest of all was a little lady, who stood at the open door of the castle; she was cut out in paper, but she had a dress of the clearest gauze, and a little narrow blue ribbon over her shoulders, that looked like a scarf; and in the middle of this ribbon was a shining tinsel rose, as big as her whole face. The little lady stretched out both her arms, for she was a dancer, and then she lifted one foot so high in the air that the Tin Soldier could not see it at all, and thought that, like himself, she had but one leg.

"That would be the wife for me," thought he; "but she is very grand. She lives in a castle, and I have only a box, and there are five-and-twenty of us in that. It is no place for her. But I must try to make friends with her."

And then he lay down at full length behind a snuff-box which was on the table; there he could easily watch the little dainty lady, who still stood on one leg without losing her balance. When the evening came, all the tin soldiers were put in their box, and the people in the house went to bed. Now the toys began to play at "visiting," and at "war," and "giving balls." The tin soldiers rattled in their box, for they wanted to join, but could not lift the lid. The Nut-cracker went head over heels, and the Pencil played games on the table; there was so much noise that the Canary woke up, and began to speak too, and even in verse. The only two who did not stir from their places were the Tin Soldier and the little Dancer; she stood straight up on the point of one of her toes, and stretched out both her arms, and he was just as firm on his one leg; and he never turned his eyes away from her.

Now the clock struck twelve—and, bounce! the lid flew off the snuff-box; but there was not snuff in it, but a little black troll; you see, it was a Jack-in-the-box.

"Tin Soldier," said the Troll; "keep your eyes to yourself."

But the Tin Soldier made as if he did not hear him.

"Just you wait till to-morrow!" said the Troll.

But when the morning came, and the children got up, the Tin Soldier was placed in the window; and whether it was the Troll or the draught that did it, all at once the window flew open, and the Soldier fell, head over heels, out of the third story. That was a terrible journey! He put his leg straight up, and came down so that he stood on his head, and his bayonet between the paving-stones.

The servant-maid and the little boy came down at once to look for him, but though they almost trod upon him they could not see him. If the Soldier had cried out, "Here I am!" they would have found him; but he did not think it proper to call out loudly, because he was in his soldier clothes.

Now it began to rain; each drop fell faster than the other, and at last it came down in a full stream. When the rain was past, two street boys came by.

"Just look!" said one of them, "there lies a tin soldier. He shall have a sail."

And so they made a boat out of a newspaper, and put the Tin Soldier in the middle of it, and he sailed down the gutter; now the two boys ran beside him and clapped their hands. Mercy on us! how the waves rose in that gutter, and how fast the stream ran! But then it had been a heavy rain. The paper boat rocked up and down, and sometimes turned round so quickly that the Tin Soldier trembled; but he was firm, and never moved a muscle, but looked straight before him, and carried his gun erect.

All at once the boat went into a long drain, and it became as dark as if he had been in his box.

"I wonder where I am going now," he thought. "Yes, yes, that's the Troll's fault. Ah! if the little lady only sat here with me in the boat, it might be twice as dark for all I should care."

Suddenly there came a great water-rat, which lived under the drain.

"Have you a passport?" said the Rat. "Give me your passport."

But the Tin Soldier kept still, and only held faster his gun.

The boat went on, but the Rat came after it. Whew! how he gnashed his teeth, and called out to the bits of straw and wood,—

"Stop him! stop him! he hasn't paid toll—he hasn't shown his passport!"

But the stream became stronger and stronger. The Tin Soldier could see the bright daylight where the arch of the drain ended; but he also heard a roaring noise, which might well frighten a bolder man. Only think—just where the tunnel ended, the drain ran into a great canal; and for him that would have been as full of peril as for us to be carried down a great waterfall.

Now he was already so near it that he could not stop. The boat was carried out, the poor Tin Soldier held himself as stiffly as he could, and no one could say that he moved an eyelid. The boat whirled round three or four times, and was full of water to the very edge—it must sink. The Tin Soldier stood up to his neck in water, deeper and deeper sank the boat, and the paper was fast dropping to pieces; and now the water closed over the Soldier's head. Then he thought of the pretty little Dancer, and how he should never see her again; and it sounded in the Soldier's ears:—

"Farewell, farewell, thou warrior brave,
Die shalt thou this day."

And now the paper broke in two, and the Tin Soldier fell through; but at that moment he was swallowed up by a great fish.

Oh, how dark it was in there! It was darker than in the drain tunnel; and then it was very narrow, too. But the Tin Soldier was firm, and lay at full length, with his gun.

The fish swam to and fro; he made the strangest stir; at last he became quite still and there was a streak of light through him. The light shone quite clear, and a voice said aloud, "The Tin Soldier!" The fish had been caught, carried to market, bought, and taken into the kitchen, where the cook cut him open with a large knife. She took the Soldier round the body with two fingers, and carried him into the room, where all waited to see the famous man who had traveled about in the inside of a fish; but the Tin Soldier was not at all proud. They placed him on the table, and there—no! What curious thing may happen in the world! The Tin Soldier was in the very room in which he had been before! he saw the same children, and the same toys stood upon the table; and there was the pretty castle with the graceful Dancer. She was still standing on one leg, and held the other extended in the air. She was faithful too. That moved the Tin Soldier: he was very near weeping tin tears, but that would not have been proper. He looked at her, and she looked at him, but they said nothing to each other.

Then one of the little boys took the Tin Soldier and flung him into the stove. He gave no reason for doing this. It must have been the fault of the Jack-in-the-box.

The Tin Soldier stood there quite in the blaze, and felt a heat that was terrible; but whether this heat came from the real fire or from love he did not know. The colors had quite run off from him; but whether that had happened on the journey, or had been caused by grief, no one could say. He looked at the little lady, she looked at him, and he felt that he was melting; but he stood firm, with his gun in his arms. Then suddenly the door flew open, and the draught of air caught the Dancer, and she flew like a sylph just into the stove to the Tin Soldier, and flashed up in a flame, and then was gone! Then the Tin Soldier melted down into a lump, and when the servant-maid took the ashes out the next day, she found him in the shape of a little tin heart. But of the Dancer was left nothing but the tinsel rose, and that was burned as black as a coal.

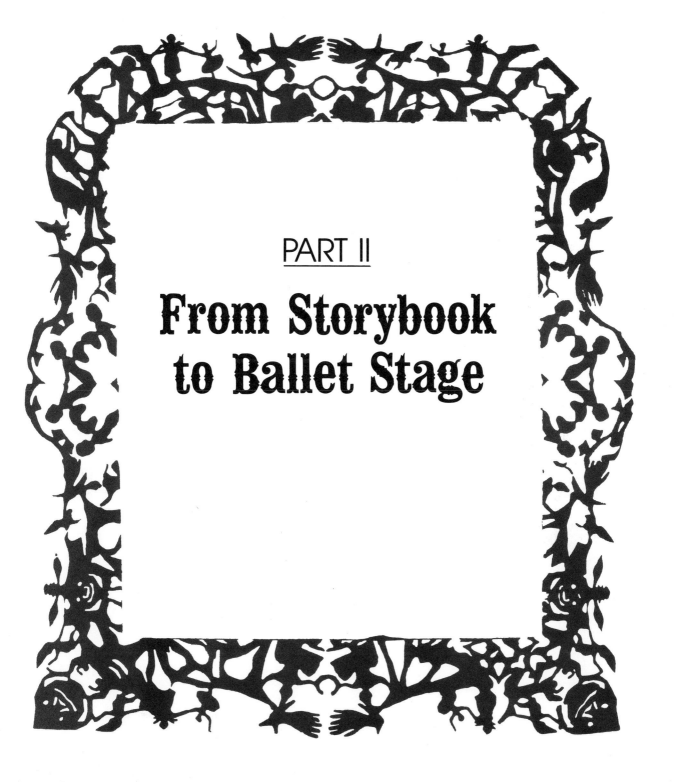

PART II

From Storybook
to Ballet Stage

THE tales of Hans Christian Andersen are a richly evocative source of inspiration for ballet choreographers. They have charm, wit, poignancy, gothic detail, period flavor, and romantic and moralistic themes — perfect elements for ballets in the narrative style. Many of Andersen's stories, moreover, deal with dance and dancers, in passing, at least, if not in any major way. This is not surprising, since the young Dane made his stage debut in a ballet called *Armida* in 1821, at the age of sixteen, and remained an avid balletomane throughout his life. In addition, he was a close, lifelong friend of the master of nineteenth century Danish ballet, August Bournonville.

Some of the tales which have been given balletic treatment over the years are *The Red Shoes, The Ice Maiden (Le Baiser de la Fée,* a ballet choreographed by George Balanchine), *The Little Mermaid, The Swineherd (Les Cent Baisers),* and, *The Steadfast Tin Soldier.* There is reference in essays on Bournonville to the fact that the choreographer felt his friend Andersen's *Tin Soldier* was danceable. However, as always in the case of transferring the subject of a work of art from one medium to another, changes are made by the artist who interprets the original. Bournonville seems to have been even more puritanical than Andersen, and felt that in his 1871 ballet, the Ballerina paper doll, with leg raised into the air was entirely too frivolous and unworthy of the Steadfast Tin Soldier's affections!

A century later, George Balanchine felt the little romance of the Tin Soldier and the paper doll Ballerina was an ideal theme for a ballet miniature. The new work, a pas de deux with oversize storybook scenery and costumes by David Mitchell, and Georges Bizet's delightful *Jeux d'Enfants* for its score, was premiered July 30, 1975, at the Saratoga Performing Arts Center, the summer home of Balanchine's New York City Ballet. It starred Peter Schaufuss, an outstanding product of the male virtuosity of the Royal Danish Ballet, then dancing with NYCB, and Patricia McBride, the superb Balanchine ballerina, who had already distinguished herself in other roles requiring the juxtaposition of doll-like animation and womanly warmth *(Harlequinade* and *Coppelia)*, and in Balanchine's distillation of his treatment of another Hans Christian Andersen tale, *Divertimento from Le Baiser de la Fée*, of 1972.

George Balanchine's *The Steadfast Tin Soldier* is a choreographic gem of demi-caractère virtuosity blended with artful sentimentality. Told by Balanchine, the tale is more tender than Andersen's; touching without bathos, amusing without silliness. The choreographer achieves this by stripping away extraneous details, characters and situations — impossible to convey satisfactorily in movement — without losing any of the story's meaning and value. In fact, the emotional impact of *The Steadfast Tin Soldier* becomes more clear and immediate.

For the most part, the story and the ballet retain the most essential elements. The biggest adjustment Balanchine has made is to give the Tin Soldier *two* legs rather than one. Andersen, as always, gives his central character some pitiful flaw or disadvantage that makes his triumph, or his failure, especially impressive, as well as symbolically obvious. Balanchine believes enough in the theme of fidelity to love and duty to give his hero two legs to stand on.

Andersen's Ballerina stands interminably on one leg, never losing her balance — a feat that leads the Tin Soldier to think that, like himself, she has only one leg, and inspires his love and admiration. Andersen's Ballerina never reveals any personality, and we never know if she notices the Tin Soldier at all. When she is blown into the flame of the stove along with the Tin Soldier, only her tinsel rose remains behind, burnt into a black coal — hardly an image to inspire tender memory. The Tin Soldier's devotion seems to have been unwise.

The Balanchine Ballerina, on the other hand, is very much aware of the soldier. We know that she is not an empty, ordinary paper doll when she expresses such joy to receive the Tin Soldier's heart and shows such tenderness when he kneels at her feet. In losing her balance all too often, showing a flexed foot at the end of a highly-extended leg, or applauding with glee for herself and her Tin Soldier, she reveals a sweetly comic side to her personality. At the same time, her dizziness hints at the ultimate destruction of this brief idyll.

By granting the Tin Soldier and the Ballerina their brief encounter, a few moments to express their love, Balanchine makes us care for them. We don't feel as emotionally involved by Andersen's characters as we are aware of their symbolic importance to the theme and moral of the tale.

Andersen illustrates the ironic twists of the story through the use of nasty hobgoblins, rats, temperamental children, and people opening doors at the wrong moment to let drafts into a room. Balanchine uses only the two central characters, lets fate take its own ironic course and leaves us with a bittersweet rather than starkly sad ending: the Ballerina is the innocent agent of her own destruction, and the Tin Soldier, left behind without his love must remain true to her by returning steadfastly to his duty at the head of his regiment.

In their individual treatments of the *Tin Soldier*, Hans Christian Andersen and George Balanchine stayed true to artistic views and motifs they reveal over and over again in their work. Andersen, with his rich narrative detail and high moral tone, reinforces the belief of his readers in their own integrity despite even the most insurmountable obstacles, or defeats. Balanchine shows, with pure choreographic craft and deft theatrical nuance, that although ideal love may be short-lived or unobtainable, one remains true to that love through dedication to duty or art. With or without analysis or interpretation of their *Steadfast Tin Soldiers*, Andersen and Balanchine provide — as they so often do — wonderfully entertaining works of imagination for the enjoyment of young and old alike.

PART III

The Ballet

The house was very still that night.
All that moved were the flames of the fire still burning in
the hearth. Suddenly — at the stroke of Midnight,
perhaps — the sound of a bright little march whispered
through the air. As the tune grew louder (but not *too*
loud), the Tin Soldier, who stood steadfastly at the head
of his regiment, began to march forward.
At first, it seemed he paraded for his own enjoyment.
But as he circled past the beautiful paper Ballerina,
standing quite still in front of the cardboard castle,
his head snapped neatly to the side to glance at her.

Did the lovely dancer in the pink dress glance back at him? The Tin Soldier couldn't quite tell.

So he showed her all his special tricks.
He trotted on his horse,

leaped into the air

to touch his toes,

turned around the floor

and spun in the air.

Did he make a good impression on her? He hoped so.
Returning to his regiment,
he saluted and waited to see.

Yes. The Ballerina had noticed him.
To a melody as sweet as your favorite lullaby, she
moved forward, stiffly at first, to dance for him.

She threw kisses from the flat-opened palms of her hands.
She rose on her toes and balanced, tipsily, since she
had probably never even moved before. She hopped back
and forth on her toes and turned on her heels,
which for a moment, made her quite dizzy.

Growing stronger, the little dancer showed the
handsome soldier how well she could stand on one leg
in several of her most difficult ballet positions.

Finally she did her very special trick:
She made *three* perfect pirouettes right in a row!

The Ballerina was

so pleased,

she couldn't help applauding for herself.

Then, the Tin Soldier gathered together all his courage . . .

... and marched to the Ballerina's side, with a salute.

She curtsied.
He bowed.

A true lady,
the dancer held out her
hand to be kissed.

. . falling to one knee
as he kissed her hand.

A true gentleman,
the soldier leaned
stiffly forward . . .

Together, they strolled arm-in-arm like sweethearts,
and the soldier was even permitted a kiss
to the lady's rouged cheek.

Their courtship was like a dream.
And, you couldn't be quite sure if
it was more of the Ballerina's twirling . . .

. . . or her great love for the Tin Soldier
that made her so dizzy that she felt rather faint.

The Tin Soldier could not wait any longer.
Kneeling at the feet of his lady, he declared his love,
asked her to marry him, then looked shyly to the floor.

The Ballerina was deeply touched.
She helped her gallant suitor to his feet . . .

. . . and together they
dreamed of their future.

She would be a happy paper doll mother;
he, a proud, steadfast tin father.

They were so happy, that they embraced . . .

. . . as tightly as her paper, and his tin, arms would allow.

As a lasting proof of his love, the Tin Soldier
reached into his uniform jacket and pulled out a perfect,
red tin heart.

"Here is my heart," he said.
"Oh, thank you! How perfect!" she replied, accepting it
from him tenderly.

The Tin Soldier then took his bride-to-be by the hand, and turned her in a promenade as she held one leg high in the air.

She curtsied. He bowed.

How happy
they were!
The Ballerina and
the Tin Soldier
hopped, galopped,
and pranced
for joy.

58

He circled around her with bounding leaps.

They bounced up into the air again and again,
laughing as they did. The Ballerina just had to
clap again and throw kisses to the far corners
of the room.

They were having such fun, it didn't seem to matter
if they woke the whole household. They danced and
danced. They linked arms, swinging each other
gaily round and round.

"Oh, what fun!" thought the Ballerina.
"But, I'm so flushed, I *must* have some air!"
Running to the tall French windows,
she threw them open wide.

"Come back!
come back!"
called the Tin Soldier,
pursuing closely
behind her
with outstretched arms.

In an instant,
a cruel gust of
wind rushed in,
tossing the
paper doll
faster and faster
into a
frantic spin
around the
room.

But, before he could catch hold of her, his beautiful love twirled on the racing draft toward the fireplace and into the leaping flames.

Like a sigh, the Ballerina was gone.
The Tin Soldier kneeled at the hearthside, wonder
in his eyes. Just a moment ago, he had known such joy.
Now he was alone.

Reaching his metal hand into the burning embers,
the soldier found all that remained of the paper doll
dancer — the red tin heart he had given to her
as a token of his love.

Kissing it, he placed the heart back under his coat,
and wiped a single tin tear from his cheek
with a white-gloved hand.

He sighed. Forlorn, the Tin Soldier marched slowly back to the head of his regiment, and sighed again.

But, remembering his duty, the soldier saluted —
perhaps not as briskly as before — then stood straight
and strong and tall.

No one would have known anything had happened
that night, were it not for a sadly empty space
in front of the cardboard castle,
and the lace curtains that now fluttered
gently in the breeze.
Only the Tin Soldier could tell what
had happened, and he stood quietly
and steadfastly still.

THE END

KEY TO PHOTOGRAPHS

Mikhail Baryshnikov, *27, 29-30, 33, 39, 41, 43* (left), *49* (bottom), *50* (bottom), *58* (bottom), *61, 67-71, 73*

Elise Flagg, *25, 31, 34-38, 42* (left), *43* (right), *44-48, 49* (top), *50* (top), *51-57, 58* (top), *59-60, 62-66*

Judith Fugate, *29*

Patricia McBride, *26, 32-33, 39-40, 42* (right), *49* (bottom), *50* (bottom), *61*

Sándor Némethy, *25, 28, 42* (left), *43* (right), *44-45, 47-48, 49* (top), *50* (top), *51-57, 58* (top), *59-60, 64-65*

Helgi Tomasson, *26*

At the time the photographs were taken Mikhail Baryshnikov, Judith Fugate, Patricia McBride, and Helgi Tomasson were members of the New York City Ballet, and Elise Flagg and Sándor Némethy were members of the Zurich Opera Ballet.